CLIMBING
THE
GREAT DENALI

By

Marie Osburn Reid

Recommended for readers age of ten-years or above.

REVIEWS

"What a GREAT ending to your wonderful adventure story! This left me choked up as well as Mitch! The emotion is so real, the way you carried us through this story, always keeping Ronnie in the story's background, but so important a part. To have it end like that was just perfect genius. I loved the whole story, the different aspects of it, and the young boys were so likeable and real as was the majestic mountain."

Adonna Marie Gipe
Author of "Songs Before Dawn"
A Collection of Traditional Love Poems
(Over 200 Love poems, published 2017)

"A great story, I was continually amazed at the courage and fortitude of these young people, facing a long, arduous and dangerous climb. I liked the technical information incorporated into the narrative, and the thoughts of Mitch as he contemplates life after 'The Climb.' The conclusion was very satisfying; it made the effort extended by the climbing team worthwhile."

Calvin Gandy
Thermopolis, Wyoming
(an author on Fanstory)

DEDICATION

This book is dedicated to my son, Mitchell Austin Ward, who is a hearty rock climber, ice climber, and a mountain climber. When he experienced Mt. Denali a second time, he made notes each day in a journal. The story is also dedicated to his climbing buddies with whom he mountaineers over the years.

CONTENTS

Acknowledgement goes to my most helpful editor who is my husband, Reford (Jeep) Reid. I appreciate my son, Mitchell Ward, for giving me his accurate details about climbing the highest mountain on the North American continent. Also, I give thanks for helpful reviews of chapters on Fanstory.

Many hundreds of years ago, Alaska natives called their biggest mountain "Denali". In 2015, Denali was ruled official for "Mt. McKinley" which was a national name after former President William McKinley

CHAPTER 1

KID WHO FIGHTS BACK

Lying in a bed before me is a child so injured in a car accident that he may never be able to walk again. A drunk driver left nine-year-old Ronnie lying in a ditch. One of his legs was so mangled it had to be amputated.

The little boy turns his head away from a teenage friend and he stares out his bedroom window. His gaze fixes a long distance away on Mt. Denali, the highest mountain in North America. Prior to 2015 it had the historic name of Mount Mt. McKinley. It was a remembrance for the past U.S. President William McKinley.

"You <u>must</u> do what the physical therapist tells you, Ronnie," I say as I park myself in a chair beside him.

"She hurts me, Mitch!" Ronnie sticks out his lower lip and has a look I remember when he was a pre-school kid. I often babysat him in those days.

He is the boy next door. Over years I taught him how to throw Frisbees, play basketball, and climb a twelve-foot climbing wall. The wall was something I built tracks on to train for rock climbing.

I wondered how to raise his spirits. His tired eyelids blinked at bright snow out the window. "You notice in March that every day is equal in daylight and darkness? That means the climbing season for Denali can begin."

Ronnie shifts a pillow and turns to me. "All you talk about is climbing the Great One. You're not old enough to go up there, Mitch."

"I'm seventeen now, and you know I do real workouts."

"Climbers fall down crevasses and freeze to death up there." Ronnie's lips curl in a sneer.

"Any climber, who puts up with some pain and lots of hard work, can get strong enough to make it all the way to the summit." I pat his thin shoulder then hold up both fists and flex the muscles in my arms.

His face lights up. "You mean you're not afraid to climb all the way up there?"

"I'm thinking about it." I put on the thoughtful look of a professor, sort of stroking my chin. "I'll consider doing it under one condition."

"What's that?" Ronnie gives me a slim, curious smile.

"There's only one thing that will get me to take on a challenge that big."

"Is there something you need?" His hazel-colored eyes open wide. "You could use my exercise ball or Dad's chin-up bars to get you in shape."

"Oh, I'm in pretty good shape. But I need one thing only you can give me."

"Denali is 20,320 feet high, Mitch. There's nothing I won't give to see you climb it."

"The big mountain will see me only if you can keep a bargain with me."

"A bargain?" Ronnie stares at me blankly, silent for a moment. "You mean you will climb if I do awful exercises? All that stuff that really hurts?"

"Well, you know climbing is hard work. It hurts to pull a sled, carry heavy stuff like food, cook stove, sleeping bag, tent ----"

His thin arms fly up. "Hike on snowshoes and pull hard on ropes to get yourself up cliffs."

"Yes, all that." I wipe my brow on my sleeve like I'm a sweating runner. "How about you? Can you keep our bargain by working hard for strong muscles?"

Ronnie glances away at the faraway peak then he turns back and looks me right in the eye. "If you do it, Mitch, would you put a flag on the top of the mountain?"

"One of those miniature Alaska flags will fit in my pocket. How about that?"

5

He stares at me for a moment. "Okay. If you try the climb, then I will try too."

I grab his hand and we do a shake followed by high-five slaps with both hands.

Mrs. Saunders enters the bedroom carrying her son's lunch on a tray. The air is filled with the smell of chicken soup. We talk for a few minutes then I shake Ronnie's hand again. Before I leave, I say to his mom, "He has big news to tell you. Ask him about the deal we made."

AsI walk back home, my Nikes crunched loudly on icy snow softening in sunlight. To call my climbing coach, Chuck Redden, I punch his number on my cell phone. He has been in Alaska less than a year but is an experienced climber. Chuck has a big desire to try a second climb on Denali. Last year he was blown off at about 16,000 feet. Strong wind kept him camped so long that he had to give up reaching the summit. He is a fireman and a certified Emergency Medical Technician whose hobby is training climbers. Chuck trains me and my buddy, Jason Harper, on frozen waterfalls and rock cliffs whenever possible. Now he will coach us into climbing Denali with real skill.

Our plan to climb Denali during the spring break at school has been in the works long before today. I neglected to tell little Ronnie the whole truth about our plan. I've been wanting to somehow make my climb encourage him to work harder to recover and walk again.

"I got everything set, Mitch," Chuck answers when his cell phone shows it's me calling. "We have bunks in Talkeetna when the train gets us there.

"Jason and I almost have the list filled that you gave us. Our backpacks are stuffed full. We'll be ready on Friday. By the way, I have a new reason for this climb." I gave him the story about Ronnie, and he reacts in a sorrowful voice.

"That poor kid. You know what? I have a friend who might help us effectively inspire little Ronnie Saunders."

"Who can do that?"

"You ever hear *Around Town with Sally,* a local news roundup on Saturday morning radio?"

"My mom turns the kitchen radio on first thing in the morning. That's a show she never misses."

"I'll give Sally a call," Chuck says and hangs up as I get to my front door.

My mother, who has the house smelling of cookies baking in the oven, anxiously asks about Ronnie Saunders and his parents. When I tell her about the bargain made between me and the kid, she surprises me with her first positive reaction to my climbing Denali.

"Well, I guess I can go along with you and your dad now that you have a fine cause. Little Ronnie needs that kind of encouragement." She puts sandwich makings on the counter and hands me a loaf of bread. Then she slips into a jacket, picks up a plate of warm cookies covered in plastic wrap, wishes me a good lunch, and heads out the door toward the Saunders' home.

On Friday, at the Alaska Railroad depot, I give both Mom and Dad hugs, and I listen to them repeat words of warning. I promise to watch out for bears, crevasses, and ice-coated cliffs. It looks and sounds like Jason is doing the same. He is surrounded by a dozen family members, two or more Alaska generations.

When Chuck shows up, we meet his radio friend. She's wearing shiny black high-heel boots, fur-trimmed parka and a puffy fur hat pulled over reddish blonde hair.

"This is Sally Johnson," Chuck says. "For her radio show she wants to carry the story of our climb for Ronnie Saunders." He introduces her to family members then she turns her shining green eyes on Jason and me.

"Glad to meet you, Mitch Warden and Jason Harper." She scribbles our names on a notepad and wears a sweet smile across a lively-looking face. "The whole town is concerned about the little boy who was almost killed by a drunk driver. I want this event to be called, *A Climb for Ronnie, The Kid Who is Fighting Back.*"

My folks and Jason's big family all bubble over with hearty comments of approval for Sally's plan, and everyone pats our backs.

The train horn blasts as Jason and I agree to keep in touch with Sally, and she vowed to tell the town that local teenagers, with Chuck, are climbing Denali.

Alaskans tend to call the high peak Denali and have even after legislators changed the name to commemorate President William McKinley. Denali is an Alaska native word meaning Great One.

Once we climb aboard the train and settle into roomy seats, Jason looks at me with a raised brow. "I remember the TV coverage when little boy, Ronnie, was struggling for life in the hospital. That reporter, Sally, is right about how the whole town cares."

Chuck smiles. "Sally also knows the town is interested when a couple of local kids like you two will be on that famous mountain. We'll be there with climbers from many states and other countries."

CHAPTER 2

CLIMBERS GET STARTED

The locomotive takes off with a jolt and squealing steel. I nearly shout, "Our climb is earlier than most isn't it, Chuck?"

Chuck nods. "Hundreds of mountain climbers favor May and June when nighttime doesn't come. They don't have to worry about it ever getting dark then.

"March, though, is a good time since day and night have even hours. Camping at night makes sleeping easier since it's dark."

"Oh yeah, I'll also find that a good time to make calls back to town," Chuck says.

13

I study the face of our climbing instructor who is nearly ten years older than Jason and me. Sun-bleached blonde hair sticks out of his knit cap and his chin is covered with stubble. He has a set of ice blue eyes that sparkled big-time when focused on Radio Sally. I make a mental note to josh him about that one day.

The railroad tracks take us over steeple-high bridges, along mountain passes, and beside frozen rivers. The country is completely bathed in purely white snow.

"I wonder what the town of Talkeetna is like," Jason says as he bites into a strip of salmon. That fish was caught and smoked by his grandparents at their fish camp on the Tanana River.

Being a Native with Alaskan ancestors from ancient times, Jason's whole life has been in the interior lands of our big state. His ambition to reach the Denali summit comes from knowing his great, great, uncle was with the first expedition known to ascend the mountain. In 1913, the Archdeacon Hudson Stuck expedition left by dogsleds from Fairbanks at St. Matthews Episcopal Church. On trails after almost two hundred miles, they reached the foot of Mt. Denali, parked the sleds, then began their climb to the summit. That took them three months. Our plan is to climb it in only a couple of weeks since we ride the train to start, then climb after landing at about 7,000 feet.

Chuck tells Jason that Talkeetna is a small town that is mostly about mountain climbing. I chime in with how fishing in the three big rivers there with my dad once, was great there too.

In the late afternoon, the train lets out sharp whistles and glides with a screech into Talkeetna. We disembark into a brisk breeze that helps sweep away the scent of the locomotive's diesel fuel. We get our packs loaded on a waiting van before the train leaves. Then it will crank up and head another hundred miles to Anchorage, a city near the mouth of the ocean.

"Look at that!" I say with my eyes drawn to the view. "We can see it all from here."

The day is clear under a perfectly blue sky. The background for the community is a whole mountain range bathed in luminous snow.

Denali stands at 20,320 feet and many lower peaks are beside it. We point out three distinctive mountains that carry names we've memorized from maps. The impressive mountains are Foraker, Hunter, and Huntington. Each presents a rugged challenge to climbers.

Jason points a hand at the view. "It's so clear. I bet that is the Ruth Gorge running up the big mountain like it does on the map."

"Yes, that is it," Chuck says. "Over there is Kahiltna Glacier running down from Mt. Foraker. That is near where our plane lands and we start the climb."

The van driver calls out, "Hey, you climbers, I'm headed for the boarding house now."

Being his only passengers, we climb into front and back seats. As the van moves down the main street, I chatter about the only other time I was there. On a warm summer day, Dad and I did a little fishing down where the big Susitna and Chulitna Rivers come together. I remember small shops, home cooking cafes, pizza and beer taverns, and a visitor center that features mountain climbing history.

"Looks like a great little town," Jason says with an eager grin.

The van pulls up to a two-story building resembling an old motel. We carry our heavy packs into the lobby and Chuck gets us checked in. The beds we get are in a long bunkroom with a row of bunks stacked two high. There are four of the bunks taken by men with a definite oriental look.

"I'm told we will share the bunkhouse tonight with a few from Japan," Chuck says.

A polite bow comes from a guest. "Ah, yes. Japan," a smiling man says. "My name is Inoki Oh."

Chuck extends a hand and shakes with all four of them. Jason and I slip in behind him and do the same. We say our names and, "How do you do?" They answer with foreign words, unfamiliar names, and cordial smiles. It turns out that the only one who speaks English is Inoki.

We bid them a good day and head outside. Our next search is for some cafe. Walking down the street the scent of pizza calls us at the very first spot. A quick meal leaves us with time to check out a shop that is well stocked with the best climbing supplies made. I buy a new plastic sled for hauling supplies from one camp to the next as we climb. Jason picks out another pair of insulated gloves.

We are settled down in the bunkhouse when darkness comes and we step outside an Aurora Borealis appears. Bright green and gold sprays dance across the sky. Chuck calls the array that shimmers by using the words mysterious, brilliant, and streaks. Jason and I laugh and call him a Cheechako. We know in is his first winter in Alaska he has seen the northern lights a few times. But we do agree this one was extra bright, truly spectacular.

Settling on our bunks, all three of us get on cell phones. Jason and I talk to parents. All we tell them is that we arrived, bedded down and will get registered as climbers with the National Park Service tomorrow morning. Chuck talks the longest and I hear him say Sally more than once.

The first thing in the morning, I make another call. "Hello there, Ronnie. I'm trying to decide if I should start climbing today or not."

"But, Mitch, why won't you start up Denali today?" Ronnie almost shouts.

"I can't go until I find out if you are keeping our big agreement. You know that's the reason I'm climbing."

"Oh." Ronnie hesitates. "Well, I was thinking about watching a new DVD today."

"Watch a movie before doing some real kicking with your nurse, Johnnie? Won't she be there?"

"She's supposed to come this morning, but I feel really tired." Ronnie sounds like a whimpering dog.

"Then a movie will just put you to sleep." I yawn loudly. "Maybe I should go back to bed and rest up too."

"Mitch, you can't do that!" I hear new energy in his voice. "All right, I guess I'll try when she gets here."

"Hey, tough guy. Do you really mean that?"

"I guess so, Mitch. At least, I'll give it a try."

"I'm going to tell Chuck and Jason that. Tomorrow we will take off in a plane, land on a glacier, and get a camp set up at 7,000-foot elevation."

"Wow, will you call me then?"

"I'll call you when I step on a glacier with crampons hitched to my boots."

CHAPTER 3

ROUTE TO CLIMB DENALI

During a big breakfast of flapjacks, eggs and bacon, our conversation is on supply talk, then centers on Ronnie's condition.

"It's tough that little kid has to figure out how to live his life after the loss of a leg," Jason says. He sadly wags his head with short-cut, coal black hair.

Chuck frowns. "I'm told a prosthetic is possible if he will put up with one and gets strong enough to make it work well. It sure is a test of his willpower."

"Yeah," I say. "Let's hope we inspire him enough, so he'll accept his physical therapist. Workouts with her can make the difference."

We gobble up breakfast then stride outdoors into crisp, calm air down to the Talkeetna Ranger Station. It opens on time at eight-thirty. They will verify our registration forms and the fees we sent in online. That way we comply with National Park Service regulations.

Inside, we line up behind the four Japanese guys from our bunkhouse. While the ranger in charge helps them, it gives us ample time to study the elaborate model of the mountain range display on a long table. Each mountain, glacier and river are molded and clearly labeled.

"That Mount Foraker looks nearly as tall as McKinley," Jason says.

A grey-haired attendant is holding a long pointer. He aims it at mountain peaks. "Yes,

Foraker is the highest peak near it. Yet, a distinctive fact is that McKinley rises a phenomenal 16,000 feet from its base. That's unlike other famous peaks in the world which are more part of mountain ranges."

After reading a nametag on the attendant's forest-green shirt, I ask, "Hey Ralph, is such a long ascent what makes Denali popular with climbers?"

Attendant Ralph nods and his older eyes deepen. "Climbers cannot resist the challenge of the long, cold trek. Almost always subzero cold and ferocious wind lashes all the way up to the peak."

"Yet, between now and mid-June, a thousand of us will climb it. Is that right?"

.

"That's likely. They come from all over the world. About half will make it to the summit, maybe more if weather cooperates." He runs his pointer along the Kahiltna Glacier. "Most climbers take this West Buttress route."

Chuck clears his throat. "Our flight is to land at the 7,000-foot level. The West Buttress route takes less time, so we are giving it a try."

"Good plan," Ralph says, and he rests his pointer on a northern route marked *Archdeacon*.

Jason's dark eyes light up. "My father's great uncle, who was native Athabascan like me, was in the expedition lead by Archdeacon Stuck."

"That means you are a descendent of Walter Harper?" Ralph lights up with surprise and reaches his hand out to Jason. "Why, he was the first man known to stand on the summit."

The ranger behind the counter lifts the paperwork that we gave him. He loudly shouts, "You must be Jason Harper."

"Yes, I'm Jason Harper."

"We are proud to see a descendent of the most famous climber, Walter Harper," says the ranger.

A burst of applause makes Jason nod and his bronze face begins to flush the color of cherries. His look of shyness gives Chuck and me a chuckle.

After clapping for Jason, the Japanese climbers finish at the counter. Moving away their enthusiasm bursts into smiles. After friendly dips of their heads, they step toward the street. Inoki pauses and says, "We fly to West Buttress. So, we might see you there."

We move up to the counter for our turn to fill out necessary paperwork with the ranger. As we finish up, the ranger pauses with intense stares at our faces one at a time. In a deep voice brimming with authority, he says, "Okay, young men, you undoubtedly know that last year two lives were lost on the mountain and that was not unusual in any year."

I take a deep breath and stare back at the baldheaded man with bushy eyebrows.

"Know that your safety is our concern. Do you understand the need to acclimate a day or so for every 3,000 feet climbed? That is one or two days of rest before moving on. Also, do you plan to dig into camp whenever a severe storm may strike?"

We answer the ranger positively. With a shake in my voice, I begin to wonder if the confidence that I show little Ronnie is beginning to vanish.

"If you have a satellite phone, you can call us if needed. It looks like you're well prepared since you list supplies including grub for about three weeks. If you are ready, Ralph will take you by the bunkhouse to pick up your gear then drive on to the airstrip. Good luck!"

We thank the ranger and Ralph leads the way to a van with the National Park Service logo on its doors. Our heavy packs and sleds are stored in the lobby, so with a few grunts, we get them stashed in the back of the van. It is a short ride to the airfield where we see light planes bearing the names of five different bush flying services.

"Which plane is ours, Chuck?" Anticipation has my head in a spin of nervous energy.

"Our reservation is with K2 Flights," Chuck announces as we stop beside a shiny red Cessna 185. The plane has skis attached to its wheels.

"This is it," says Ralph. "I wish you well."

"Thank you, Ralph," we say. I notice Jason's voice is a screechy shrill. I never heard his usual calm way change to that before.

We pull our things off the van, and it drives away.

"Can that little plane be big enough?" I ask and plop down my pack, thinking of how it weighs at least sixty pounds.

A man, dressed in leather and a captain-beaked hat, hustles toward us. "Hello there guys. This is our smallest plane, but just right to fly you three up to the strip on Kahiltna Glacier. I'm Duke Mills, your pilot today."

We tell him our names, and Chuck hands him a camera. The pilot snaps a photo of us beside the plane then he poses for a shot with me and Jason.

After Chuck clicks the camera a few more times, Duke instructs us on how he wants each piece of our gear packed on board. As soon as that's done, Jason and I fasten our seatbelts in back seats. Chuck takes advantage of his seniority and settles in the seat beside the pilot.

The engine roars to life in mild thirty-degree sunshine. Duke hands us each a headphone. On it I hear our pilot Duke and voices from other planes in the area.

While Duke carefully goes through his preflight checklist, he shouts, "I'm guessing this is your first climb up the Great One."

Jason and I say yes with enthusiasm.

"Well, remember if severe weather blocks your way, come on down. Don't risk more than that summit is worth."

"We'll see to it," answers Chuck and he explains how horrific winds kept him from reaching the summit last year.

The engine revs up and the plane slides on skis down the taxiway, passing hangars and parked planes. Once on the runway, Duke pulls the throttle and the plane accelerates on skis, then lifts smoothly into the air. We are aloft over vast open country.

Frozen rivers below appear as winding white ribbons and dark green spruce trees are the only color in the snow-covered land. As our plane climbs above hills and jagged rock cliffs, up ahead the great mountain looms closer and closer. We fly so low that mountain ridges rise above us on both sides of a path formed by a glacier. Before long, we view the frozen glacier as a well-used landing strip. Kahiltna Glacier spreads ice over a huge expanse.

"This is it," the pilot announces as he gently sets the plane down on the ancient flow of ice and taxis to a side of the runway then stops. He leans back in his seat with the heater blowing warm air and watches us pull on gloves, zipper up coats and tie down hoods.

"You're at 7,300 feet. The summit will give you a battle for another 13,000 feet," he hollers with a smile.

The engine stays running as we jump down into a sharp wind that sweeps a fine dust of snow around us. Having left temperatures above freezing, then landing here on a minus-twenty-degree day makes our cheeks and fingers sting with cold.

"It's definitely winter here," I call out.

We unload the plane and shout thanks to Duke. He yells back, "Give me a call when you're down off the mountain and I'll come after you. That is, if weather permits. Good luck."

"Wow, all I see is a field of snow," Jason says. "I've never seen a glacier so huge."

"Denali looks a whole lot bigger than I ever imagined," I say. "Feels like a country all its own, doesn't it?"

All three of us stand still and watch the red Cessna taxi back up the runway. It turns and takes off into the wind like a hero roaring away. Seeing the plane fade into a small speck under the blue sky and its sound die away, felt like it abandons us in a white world of silence.

CHAPTER 4

INTO THIN AIR

Luckily, the wind begins to ease off and so does the chill factor. The sun gleams off streaks of blue ice in the glacier that has lain frozen for thousands of years. The Kahiltna Glacier flows down the mountain as a frozen river and is a half-mile wide. In ancient downhill progress, a labyrinth of crevasses formed, and many became hidden under veils of snow.

Chuck says, "Let's strap on snowshoes, rope ourselves together, and get up the glacier beyond the airstrip."

"And set up Base Camp," I say, proud to use a climbers' term.

To get ready to hit the trail, we attach supply sleds to our waist belts to drag. Snowshoes will keep us on top of soft snow rather than having to trudge through deep drifts. With our heavy backpacks on, we get roped together at about thirty feet apart. The rope is one with a lot of stretch so the distance between us will vary depending on how much pull is put on it.

"I'll take the lead," Chuck says. "You two keep eyes peeled for crevasses."

I line up next behind Chuck. "Kahiltna is so vast we'll be stomping in snowshoes all afternoon, and right now I'd say it looks mellow."

Jason stops to adjust his sun goggles. "Oh sure, Mitch, mellow if we can spot solid ice bridges over a crevasse or two."

Tied together, we head across the glacier. We stop at a slice in the glacier that is no more than three feet wide but looks bottomless down its blue-black sides. Here there is no such thing as a snow bridge. After giving it a thorough examination, we agree to jump it. With snowshoes pulled off, I'm first with my backpack on and Chuck belays me with a harness and figure-eight clasp that can stop my fall if the edge of the crevasse tumbles off. It feels like an easy hop when I hit the other side.

Chuck and Jason toss the sleds one at time over for me to catch and anchor. Then I belay those guys across one at a time. Standing safely across that scary, deep crevasse is a good feeling.

By mid-afternoon, we happily park the sleds at a site where other climbers have once dug in. Chuck pulls his GPS out of a pocket. "Ah, we made our first goal. We're at 7,900 feet."

"So, no more hiking today?" I ask. Glad to dump my heavy pack, I stretch and rotate my arms. Exertion on snowshoes and pulling a load leaves my body-skin sprinkled with sweat despite frigid air.

"A tour of the area to look for a danger or two won't hurt us," Chuck says.

"And we need to adjust for the higher altitude," Jason says. "We are up about 7,000 higher than we were in Talkeetna."

"Begin acclimation by doing a loud deep-breathing exercise," Chuck said, and so we did.

To set up our base camp we hollow out a space in the snow where we can put up the tent against slab walls, a good shield from wind. After the tent is in place, we fill it with sleeping bags and gear.

Jason unpacks our one-burner cooker and gets snow boiling for drinking water. As an EMT, Chuck tells us to drink three quarts a day and to stuff down food. I know for sure that munching on power bars all day is not enough. The scent of cooking dehydrated food in a pressure cooker invites me to eat, even if it lacks the taste of Mom's home cooking.

By evening and another good snack, we are ready for a night's rest. The night is dark with moonbeams behind the huge mountain causing it to loom as a silhouette. Pure silence becomes a reality without our snowshoes crunching through snow, or our gulps for oxygen in steep spots, or our hustle to set up the tent.

Jason breaks the silence when he tunes his radio to an Anchorage radio station. I let scratchy music wash over me as I curl up inside my warm bag. I try to read by flashlight, but the long day that started in Talkeetna and ended on the glacier puts me to sleep in an instant.

****

"Hey, we're buried in frost," Jason bellows when bright sunlight hits in the morning.

I'm shocked to see the ceiling and walls lined with hoarfrost. The thick, sparkling layers are put there by our warm, moist breath. Frost has built up through the night.

42

"Let's get up and cover our bags," Chuck says. "We need to scoop out all the frost before the sun puts enough heat on the tent to melt it."

"We sure don't want our bags wet," I say and follow his lead by spreading my Gore-Tex jacket over my sleeping bag. With gloves we scrape down the frost onto coats, scoop it up and empty it outside. That's the first activity to begin the day.

Later in the morning, my call to Ronnie misses him. His father tells me the little guy and his wheelchair are loaded in the car and they are off to see doctors.

I hand the satellite phone to Chuck, and he does get through to Radio Sally. Exactly where we are sounds tough for him to explain as he repeats the name of the glacier, the elevation, and what mountains we see from here. Then he gives her a report on our weather saying that a hard wind in the night covered our tents and sleds with snowdrifts. He says, with good vision this morning, we should make it to 11,000 feet today. That's what he tells so she can broadcast all the details. But some of his remarks sure don't seem to be about trekking the glacier, nor about Jason and me. He stomps away from our stares with his back turned so we can't see blue eyes twinkling.

Before the satellite phone hits his pocket, I ask, "How come that gal only talks to you? She doesn't ask for me or even Jason."

"It must be that Sally cares only about you, Chuck," Jason says with a grin.

Chuck's lips curl a little and he gives a wordless stare at us then at the mountain. "Let's get going today with snowshoes until the surface gets more of a crust," he says, sounding like the boss on a job.

The temperature is up to twenty degrees. We rub on sunblock lotion to keep away 'glacier burn'. We rope up together and set out for a long day ahead. Our big boots plod cautiously across snowfields on the glacier. The route takes us around a deep pocket of caves built by snow slides and wind, yet it looks like outer-space creations.

While our progress is steady, we take breaks for snacks and water canteens. By the time the setting sun begins to turn our world of white to hues of red and gold, we make it to the 11,000-

foot level. There we find a surprise. Not far away we see two bright yellow tents nestled in a snowbank.

"Hey, that must be the Japanese climbers," Jason says. "One of them is skiing over here."

"I wish we brought skis," I say. "Look how fast he moves."

Chuck waves as the skier poles his way up to us. "Hello, how's everyone in your party doing?"

"Doing good." The climber's Japanese accent is mixed with puffing breath. "We stay for three days. We do many short climbs in this area. Good for our breath."

"We'll stay here too, Inoki, and get well adjusted to the altitude," Chuck says so loudly I figure he is showing off for remembering the name of the one who speaks English.

Jason and I tell Inoki hello. He cordially responds with a bow of his head then he aims his skis out into the setting sun and slides away.

Chuck pulls a short shovel off a sled and hands it to me. I get busy and dig out a nice size bowl with tall banks to give our tent wind protection for the next couple of days. As high calorie noodles respond to the flame of a one-burner cooker, fog in the form of a billowing cloud sweeps down from Kahiltna Pass. In minutes, the yellow tents that are less than a football field away cannot be seen.

"Hey, every mountain peak has disappeared." I look around feeling astonished to see the ground wrapped in a cloud.

"Think that skier, Inoki, can find his way back to his buddies?" Jason asks.

"I'm sure he headed back as soon as he saw fog rolling in," Chuck says. "Like us, they had better stick right here."

****

For the rest of this day and all the next, we barely leave our campsite. There in the middle of a thick cloud, I get creative. Me and Jason, with our axes and knives get to work. On a slab of ice, we sculpt out "O ZONE" in clear letters and mount it as a camp sign.

As the second day drifts by, tired muscles feel strong again. Huffing and puffing in the thin air gets easier and slight dizziness fades away. I decide it's true that it takes time to acclimate.

On a call to Ronnie, I ask how his exercises are going.

"Johnnie tells me not to be a whiny butt."

I laugh. "Why's that?"

"She makes me lift weights."

"Oh, did that make you a whiny butt?"

"Well, sort of. But yesterday I did the two-pounders."

"I'll bet that makes your arms feel stronger now. Right?"

"I think so, Mitch. Maybe I can get strong again."

"Super, Ronnie. You sure don't sound like a whiny butt anymore!"

CHAPTER 5

TUMBLE INTO A CREVASSE

We awake to breezy sunshine and frost-covered walls in our tent. After scraping down hoarfrost and then getting a belly full of cooked oatmeal, we pack up for a long day of hiking.

"Chuck, for trekking up to the new camp, can I take a try at the lead?"

"Well, Mitch, you're a guy who's always in a hurry. Can you be cautious enough to use the probe to locate hidden crevasses? You got to know when the route is solid."

"No problem." I stomp my snowshoes on the firm glacier. "This hard ice is on thousands of feet of snow that packed here in billions of centuries."

"Lead the way, Mitch." Jason snorts and clips onto the rope extending 60 feet behind Chuck and me.

Sleds filled with our supplies are harnessed to our waists. There is a pull hard on hip muscles as we trudge up a sharp incline. For over a couple of hours I probe a ski pole into the surface. That is to make sure the trail is solid.

There are scenic wonders around us, and when we stop to catch a breath and eat a snack, I point at an ice fall ahead that swoops above us in astounding flows. Amazing Mt. Foraker and Mt. Crosson illuminate before us capturing my attention. They make me wonder about what mysteries lay ahead in climbing Denali.

Two pairs of big ravens with bushy black wings fly in from a cliff of jagged rock. They caw loud greetings. That is the only wildlife seen.

Looking at birds and mountains distract me for a horrific moment. I'm hit with a terrifying shock as my ski pole plunges through the surface. My whole body follows it. I tumble into darkness.

The rope stretches tight and stops my fall with a jolt. I yell a loud scream. I figure it is no doubt that Chuck and Jason have reacted like experts. They must have dug in their ice axes to stop the fall. The full weight of the loaded sled dangles from me and bangs against both walls of the narrow crevasse. I'm suspended at least twenty feet from the top of a bottomless ice pit. I push off my sun-goggles and stare at deep blue ice walls.

My hands and feet seem to shake. I force myself to take a deep breath. Not willing to look down into vast darkness, I focus on ice walls lined with white rims of snow.

My buddies hidden from view yell, "Mitch you okay?"

"The rope is holding. I can climb out," I shout, but deep walls drown out the sounds. I assume they can't hear me. At least the stretched rope is holding.

Even with shock running from my toes to my head, I know it's not likely they can pull the rope up. The weight of me and the sled is too heavy for that. I get ready to try a steep climb.

My ice axe unclips easily from my belt, and I sink it into the ice wall. Gripping it, I steady myself against the sheer wall enough to unhitch the sled that pulls hard on my hips. I let the sled dangle on the rope. I pull one snowshoe off my foot and hitch it to the rope, then do the same for the other foot.

"You're held tight," Chuck calls out, sounding a mile away.

"Climb, Mitch, climb." Jason's shout sounds as faint as a whisper.

To lighten my load more, I get my backpack tied onto the rope then slip it off my shoulders. From the pack I pull out well-spiked crampons. Attached on my boots I manage to get my feet fit ready for ice climbing. I dig the sharp spikes into ridges on the cliff. With the ax embedded securely, I take a step upward following our security rope that's stretched tight.

Climbing frozen waterfalls has been my favorite sport, but a fall from one of them has always meant hitting soft snow. This is very different. I look up toward blue sky and fight against fear. I pray the rope won't give away and let me tumble down the crevasse to its invisible bottom.

I stab one toehold at a time into the frozen wall and reset the ax deep. It supports me. This is the climb of my life. I'm certain that it will take all my effort to reach the top. Only that can save my life. Here in an ice world, perspiration runs off my brow and down my back.

I have a vision of little Ronnie struggling to move arms and his one remaining leg. That thought forces me to use all my strength. I inch up with each step wedged against solid ice. I force the ax to dig in higher with each step, and I hang on to seek out the next foothold. Gradually the white crust of snow framing the blue sky gets closer.

Eventually, I see the best thing ever. Chuck's gloved hand appears over the precipice and reaches down. My arm stretches up until we touch. He grabs my wrist. With a big grunt he yanks me over the top.

I scramble onto snow and wallow on a solid crusty surface with my trembling legs dancing in the air. Chuck and Jason jab happy hands and I wonder which of us is the most relieved.

"Got any strength left?" Jason asks.

I wobble my head up and down then push my sun goggles down over my eyes against the snow-blinding glare. My voice seems to have disappeared until I have a thought. "My ski pole's gone." I sit up. "I think I heard it bounce off ice-walls and, before I heard you shout, there was a plunk sound that echoed."

"That pole is buried in ancient ice." Jason poses with his hands together in prayer as if at a gravesite.

"Okay, let's drag that sled up before we starve!" Chuck grabs hold of the rope that is securely anchored to ice screws.

"Yeah," I say, anxious to save our groceries. The jitters inside me bring thoughts of food. I get up on wobbly feet and dig my crampons in beside the rope.

We all pull together as Chuck calls, "One, two, three, pull! One, two, three, pull!"

Our tugs finally bring my backpack and the heavy sled up onto the glacier. Seeing them under sunlight, I figure my battle with that dark icy hole is over.

Under the clear sky, we cook up a good lunch and nestle into a comfy snowbank. It feels good to relax tense muscles that had worked hard to save my life. I bow my head in thoughts of thanks until the buzz of a motor fills the silence. The sound grows loud as a plane makes circles above us. We're sure It is bringing in more climbers or showing off mountains to tourists. We give it a good wave then jump up and get on our way.

Chuck says, "Leave crampons on. This surface is crusty, no need for our snowshoes now."

As Jason straps snowshoes to his sled, he throws Chuck a sly look. "Don't let Mitch be the leader."

I give out a moan.

Together both Chuck and Jason say, "Don't be a whiny butt!"

Joining their thoughts of little Ronnie, I laugh.

Chuck announces, "I'll lead us to the next campsite."

CHAPTER 6

RELAYS ON THE GLACIER

While daylight hours last, we manage to settle into camp just under the 13,000-foot level. As the setting sun casts endless shadows over mountains and tints them in colors, my thoughts turn to Ronnie. I think of how he spent so many weeks in a coma then awakened with strength drained from his injured body. Worst of all, the loss of his leg left him with no will to get back into action. He was more like a sick puppy, content only to lie about and not care to be a nine-year-old boy again. Somehow, his bargain with me about climbing Denali hit a spark. I visualize him lifting the weights he mentioned and wonder if he's making an effort to pull himself upright or trying to stand yet.

I ask Chuck for the satellite phone and the signal is strong, so I dial. Mrs. Saunders answers with a tear in her voice. "Ronnie's not doing well today. He took a fall. Hold on, I'll let you talk to him, Mitch."

"Hello, Mitch," says a listless voice.

"Hey, kid. What's that your mom says about taking a fall?"

"Mean Johnnie made me hang on and stand by myself. I can't do that with just one leg. It's too hard."

"Well, Ronnie, I know what you're talking about. I took a big fall today, too." I gave him all the details of my tumble into the crevasse and the labor it took to pull myself up the ice wall.

"Wow, you worked really hard to get to the top?"

"I did, and what made me come up one foot at a time was thinking about you. I could just see you having as big a battle as me."

"If you didn't climb out, you would fall to the bottom. Then you would be dead, Mitch." His voice perks up.

"And if you give up, Ronnie, where will you be?"

"I guess, just here in bed."

"All the time? Is that the way you want it?"

"Heck, no, but……"

"You got a fight as big as climbing out of a crevasse and scaling up a mountain. It takes sticking with it."

"Yeah, I guess that's right." Courage flows into the sound of his words.

"Remember our deal, Ronnie. If you choose to give up, I've got to come off the mountain right away."

"You got to keep going, Mitch, so you can get the flag up to the summit."

"Ah, then you'll give a good workout with Johnnie tomorrow?"

"Okay, I will."

When I hang up, Jason asks how the kid is doing. I repeat little Ronnie's words and we both feel encouraged. Chuck hears none of it. His ear is glued to the satellite phone. We hear him give

Radio Sally the details of our plan tomorrow on how we will carry supplies a little at a time up to a new campsite. Then he walks out into the night leaving Jason and me with no ears for his further comments.

We get out a deck of cards and as we try some Blackjack, Jason goes into great-detail describing the fear and dread he felt when I took the big tumble. I could only thank him for his super quick effort that helped stop my fall.

My last thoughts for the night were full of giving thanks.

****

The next day begins at twenty-five degrees below zero. We get moving early on our fifth day atop Kahiltna Glacier. The slope seems fairly gentle, but most of the terrain is about to change. Now it will turn steeper, which makes heavy loaded sleds slide easily. Also, slanting up a sharp incline, the harness on the sled will tug hard on our hips and legs. That could give us sore muscle.

We decide to make a base camp at slightly below 13,000 feet. This will be a good place to store sleds and supplies we will need later. Doing that, we can carry some supplies up the steeper climb then return later for more. We bury gear deeply in snow to outsmart Ravens that may fly by. Those big, smart birds are likely to poke their beaks through snow and rip into our supplies.

Chuck jabs a wand bearing our names into the pile. "There, we can find our extra gear when needed, and it's deep enough so other campers will know too."

"Brrr, that wind getting stronger should keep ravens away," says Jason. He tucks cold fingers under armpits and stomps his feet.

I do the same, anxious to start climbing so my body can generate heat all the way from my facemask to my socks. With fully loaded backpacks, our climb will take us to a new campsite. Roped together we jab our crampon boots in crusty snow, one step after another, on a steep grade.

When we take a break, we flop onto the snow, breathe deeply, and snack on power bars. Under the clear sky, we gaze at ridges fronting our route and a white panorama of mountains that surround us.

I point a pole at where a harsh breeze blows spurts of snow. "Is that the spot called Windy Corner that was on the map, Chuck?"

"It is, and like a funnel against the West Buttress, it creates its own high velocity wind."

"That's Sultana," Jason yells out and points at the nearby mountain. "It's the wife to Denali."

I squint through goggles at blowing snow that swirls before a towering peak. "Yeah, it's Mt. Foraker," I say and smile at the way Jason likes to tell Athabascan names for mountains and what they mean. I pull out my camera and give it a couple of clicks. "From here it looks fantastic."

The campsite we want is just over the Kahiltna Pass, so we duck our heads into a high wind and press on. Climbing hard in slow steps takes us up more than another 2,000 feet. Once there, we empty our packs and stash supplies in a dug-out spot. Now we must return to the base camp to get more supplies.

With empty backpacks, we slide on our butts down the steep slope and dig ice axes into the snow to keep speed under control. It takes only minutes to slip and scoot back down to the base camp. We giddy, laughing guys sound like kids playing in the snow. But then we get to work refilling backpacks and start uphill again.

A total of three hikes up then down, make it a long, tough day. Once we camp for the night, we're more than ready to dig deeper walls and set up the tent where it will be protected from extreme wind. On this side of the pass, we're out of the strongest wind.

Once we're set up, we feast on hot noodles boiled in melted ice shavings. Our phone can't lock onto a satellite. No calls get through.

"Hey, Chuck, that gorgeous radio gal is missing your call tonight," I say when we settle in warm bags under the tent.

"I never suspected you thought of Sally as a pretty girl," Chuck says.

"Yeah, we noticed. Right, Jason?"

In twilight filtering into the tent, Jason's dark, sleepy eyes peek out of his down bag. "Well, I could tell Chuck really, really noticed pretty."

"Yeah, it shows, Chuck," I say.

Chuck's feet inside his bag give me a sharp jab. "Good night, you two."

Jason and I chuckle.

Darkness puts our tired bodies to sleep fast.

****

It seemed no more than five minutes when I wake up to a morning filled with sunshine. Looks like a perfect day for climbing, but we won't. Today is for acclimation. We clear away a buildup of hoarfrost in the tent then stuff ourselves with pancakes.

The silence is broken by two circling airplanes and to an Anchorage radio station that barely comes in. We do some hiking and take pictures of each other. By late afternoon, we marvel at a glacier slab that juts to about seventy feet high and at least a hundred feet long. It has a knife-edged ridge and sheer drop into a crevasse on the other side. I take a lot of spectacular pictures.

Back in camp we figure out what food and fuel we need to pack up to 17,000 feet. I tend the fire to cook more water and notice something in the distance. "Way down there, it looks like climbers." I point at the ridge we scaled yesterday.

"They're wearing bright yellow parkas, just like the Japanese team," Jason says. "It looks like they are heading to set up camp higher tonight."

"Likely they'll get stronger wind another thousand feet up along that rim. There's not as much protection like we have at this embankment," Chuck says. We wave our arms when they're a little closer, and they wave back but don't hesitate in climbing.

The night sky fills briefly with dancing lights that swirl directly above in a moonless sky. When the awesome aurora fades, we end a star-filled night with Jason's cards. I become a loser in every hand of playing Hearts.

CHAPTER 7

MOUNTAINEERING

I wake up and poke my head out of the tent. Only a dim trace of morning sun comes through a cloud enveloping us. Above snores that fill the tent, I holler, "Our route is invisible. Even the mountain disappeared."

"Oh no. You sure, Mitch?" Chuck groans.

"Pure fog!" I sling on my parka and step out to answer the call of nature.

"In that case, we'll go nowhere today." Our leader sighed.

That is a letdown. More than two days of hanging around here at 14,200 feet will make us restless.

A sleepy moan out of silence comes from Jason. "Call when you get water boiling for oatmeal. No way do I get up 'til then."

"Okay, Skinny," I call. He does look like he has gotten leaner. Physical demands are immense when carrying heavy backpacks in increasing altitude. It seems impossible to follow Chuck's orders to stuff up on enough food and drink quarts of water. My appetite drops too, so I tighten my belt.

The covering cloud immerses us in a warm twelve degrees above zero, so cooking without gloves is a treat. A propane scent lingers in the still air when I get the burner fired up. Scoops of clean snow take time to boil. I add oatmeal and get it cooked until thick then I carry the pot into the tent before it cools off. I stick three spoons in it and we eat out of the pot with heaps of sugar.

Strains of music, voices, and static come from Chuck's radio. He flips back and forth through stations and anxiously checks his watch.

"Hey, Chuck, does the time matter?" Jason asks with a mocking smile.

"It matters to get the right station. *Around Town with Sally* broadcast will be on in a couple of minutes."

"Oh, so today is Saturday?" I'm amazed to think I could lose track of what day it is.

"If there's no big news, she may mention our climb this week," Chuck says, sounding like he's glad we can't go hiking off.

A male announcer's voice comes through. "*Around Town with Sally* comes up after this message." Impatiently we wait while a parade of ads for pickup trucks, chewing gum, pizza, and vitamins fall on our ears before Sally's voice flows in.

"Greetings to all in Fairbanks and the Tanana Valley. Let me fill you in on this week's happenings with the Mayor, City Council and Wildlife Services. Then, finally the latest on our story, *A Climb for Ronnie, The Kid Who is Fighting Back*."

"She is going to talk about us," Jason says with shining eyes.

"I wonder if she knows what progress Ronnie is making," I say as she makes comments about the city mayor.

Chuck nods. "She told me about a visit with the kid." He holds a shush finger on his lips, so Jason and I settle in to listen.

I half hear the details of a city ordinance to increase the fine for littering, then stuff about a wildlife plan to clear a field of snow for spring arrival of geese and ducks. More ads come next. Finally, Sally's cheerful voice returns with, "Chuck Redden leads two Fairbanks teenagers, Mitch Warden and Jason Harper, up Denali to the 14,000 level so far."

Sally gives details about how we are the first Alaskan climbers to attempt Mt. Denali this year. She mentions our high school, and that Chuck Redden is an E.M.T. fireman with extensive mountaineering experience who is eminently qualified to lead our team. "These three climbers are an inspiration to Ronald Saunders, a nine-year-old who lost a leg in an accident months ago and is still bedridden. When I saw Ronnie this week, he told me that Mitch had fallen into a deep crevasse but had bravely climbed out. The boy said it made him believe that if he keeps working to recover then someday he will. Ronnie Saunders thanks all our audience for cards and letters sent to wish him well and success to his mountaineering buddies."

A sports reporter takes over, so Chuck clicks off the radio to save on the battery. I see a faraway look in his eyes. Then I look at Jason and know they are both as choked up as I am. "Isn't that neat that people are actually sending cards?"

"Sally has a good program, Chuck," Jason says as he turns away and searches his bag for fresh socks to warm his feet.

"Yeah, she sure does." Chuck drawls out those words like a ballad singer with more than a drop of admiration.

Jason looks at me and we share grins.

After a search through pockets, I locate my cell. I get no signal at this height on the mountain, so I switch to the satellite phone. Dialing Ronnie's number gets only an answer-machine. I say, "We heard the show *Around Town with Sally* and it sounds like all of Fairbanks is rooting for you, Ronnie. I'll call back later."

The rest of the foggy day, I take advantage of the mild temperature and cut a slab of ice for a sculpture. I work hard to carve out a bear, but Jason decides it looks like a fat dog. He helps me move it to a spot that shows Fat Dog sniffing what's cooking in our camp.

****

Sculpting felt good and I notice staying a full three days at this altitude renews my energy and all feeling of muscle strain goes away. Jason and Chuck agree they feel stronger too.

The sun bursts through in late afternoon and exposes the mountain above. The clouds that covered our camp slip below us and block out hills and valleys. A mysterious, awesome sensation comes over me as I look down the mountain into nothing but clouds. The whole world becomes obscure as if we are high up above it all.

"Cartoon angels walk on clouds," I tell Chuck and Jason. Together we gaze down at puffy, white clouds. Nods from them make me know they, too, feel the vanished world below seems unreal.

With a shrug, Chuck says, "Here's a big treat for supper." He digs into dinner supplies and pulls out the oversized can of chili beans that he insisted on packing all the way up.

Our day ends right after dinner and a few games of cards. We resolve to rise earlier tomorrow and attack an even steeper climb -- if the weather holds.

****

All three of us sleep soundly until a sharp morning light pierces the tent. The sky is mostly blue with no more than thin patches of clouds.

Sun-soaked ice crystals look like sparkling diamonds that swirl around us in a light breeze.

In a mild fifteen-degree temperature we scurry around to get supplies that are well buried under snow.

Jason heaves straps over his shoulders. "Ugh," he grunts. "My backpack weighs at least sixty pounds,"

"We need it all to get up the next really treacherous slope," Chuck says. "That's close to the point where wind stopped me last year."

Exhilaration pours through me. "If we make it to the 17,200-point today, our next climb after will be to the top of the summit."

Jason shouts, "Right on man! Let's do it!"

As we clip on the rope that links us, Chuck asks me to lead. He must think I've learned my lesson against crevasses. Feeling proud and determined to make the right steps this time, I jab in a probe and move out.

Our route is a steep section that reveals a choice of two iffy snow bridges spanning across a crevasse. Craggy edges run the entire length up the slope. The snow bridge I choose looks the stronger. With each careful step I probe deeply with my pole. It feels solid. Glad we're well strapped together. I make it across. Chuck and Jason follow me safely. I let out a breath of relief.

Now, we move almost purely vertical. After every ten to fifteen feet up the slope, the altitude forces us to stop for a rest. It's important to catch deep breaths. Also, because we climb with toes pointed out like ducks walk, I need to rest my aching ankles.

The next slope is even steeper. After a total of six hours climbing, we make it to the 16,400-level and exhaustion is what we feel the most. We're at a flat section of a ridge with plenty of room, but there are sharp drop-offs on each side.

I sprawl out on the snow and stare up at something that is not white. A multitude of earth tones shape an overhanging, jagged rock. "This is a great spot. I propose we camp right here."

Chuck gives my boot a kick. "What? Mitch, you were predicting another thousand feet higher."

Jason flops down beside me. "I don't think I can go another ten feet."

"Okay, look up there." Chuck points upwind. "A big snow-cloud is descending. Let's get camp set up before the white stuff falls."

In a fast dig we encircle a spot surrounded by walls of snow, but the cloud is faster and reaches us with dense snow flurries. Wind picks up so both Jason and I work together to keep the burner going to cook a hot pasta dish, or so it says on the package. We melt lots of snow and ice for water to drink. In a short while, Chuck gauges the wind at forty miles an hour. The cold wind whips at our tent, but the anchors set into deeply dug-out walls keep the tent from blowing open.

After dinner and a quick cleanup, we are in a scramble to get into warm sleeping bags as early as possible. I manage to get a call to Mom and

Dad, but the connection clicks off after only a few words. My most welcome thought is that a good rest will be possible right here. We won't continue climbing until the weather clears. Glad for rest, I slip into a deep sleep.

****

The sound of roaring wind is gone in the morning. I jump out of bed, but neither Chuck nor Jason moves a muscle. I resolve to make pancakes, but first I give in to a big urge to climb the rock ridge above us. I take my camera to capture one of those panoramic views. I make it up there in a few minutes and edge my way out on the overhang. I perch on the hard rock surface like a king of the mountain, fill my lungs with crisp air and pull my camera out of a warm pocket. The lens focuses on spectacular mountains, the narrowing Kahiltna Glacier, and rocks jutting out of ice. I snap away until I see something move.

The motion is only a football field away. I can see yellow tents peek through sprinkles of new snow and one guy is moving around.

"Ho!" I yell and wave. The sound of my greeting fills the silent world. A familiar Japanese man raises a hand and starts hiking towards me.

I scuttle off the boulder, plant my boots, and make hasty tracks across the glacier. It's not a long run, but the high altitude has me panting like an old dog. We meet halfway between our two camps. When I get a good look at him, I'm relieved to see it is the one who speaks English well. I reach out my hand. Our gloves meet for a good shake, but he doesn't return my smile. His face is wrinkled with worry lines.

"How goes it, Inoki?" I ask.

"Good, until yesterday. Looks like our buddy Nomo is a sick man. I don't know what we will do."

"Chuck can be a big help. He is a certified E.M.T. Come on up and have hotcakes with us. He can talk to you at our camp."

CHAPTER 8

SICKNESS STRIKES

Up at 16,400 feet, our camp hides behind the immense rock ridge. Inoki and I first notice a mouthwatering scent. It is hotcake batter. With a big spoon, Jason is whacking in a bowl full of flour mixed in water.

I loudly announce Inoki, then tell about how I spotted his camp from a perch on the overhanging rock.

"I heard you hollering. That's what got me up," Jason says as he shakes hands with Inoki.

Chuck quickly comes out of the tent, greets Inoki, and reaches out a bare hand.

"Our man Nomo is feeling ill. I worry for him," Inoki says. "I am told you are a trained Emergency Medical Technician."

Chuck nodded. "I can check on him. We saw your team pass our last camp a couple days ago, so it looks like you've been acclimating here for a while."

"We delayed here. Hope Nomo will feel better."

I point past the ridge. "Their camp isn't far. But don't leave 'til we chow down."

"Here's a stack," Jason calls. His spatula flops slightly charred pancakes onto a sheet of foil paper.

I hand Inoki a fork, a square of foil to use for a plate, and set out a bottle of syrup. He grins and bows politely then settles against the dugout wall. I see he, too, has a dark suntanned face. The temperature is a mellow twenty-five degrees and an intense sun beams down on us.

Conversation bubbles over with climbing details and strong yearnings to reach the summit. Shortly we all set out for Inoki's camp.

"Here comes wind with a bitter bite," I say.

"Looks like clouds are pushing in over Sultana," Jason says and turns to Inoki. "That is the Athabascan name for the mountain closest to Denali. On maps it's Mt. Foraker."

"I see two of your teammates headed toward us," I say when I spot puffy hooded jackets and knitted hats embroidered with Japan's orange sun.

When they reach us, Inoki asks us to pronounce our names for them. Then he carefully pronounces their names. To myself I recite Eri and Taiko over-and-over, so I get the right name on the right guy.

They tell us Nomo is resting. We all start walking to reach their campsite. Coughing is heard from one of the tents. Inoki and Chuck immediately enter the tent.

"I thought we were in germ free mountains. That makes me wonder how he caught a cold," Jason says.

"Remember we read climbers can get altitude sickness?" I say, and Jason agrees.

Digging in supplies, Taiko pulled out a cellophane package. "You cookies," he says in limited English and offered a pack of thin wafers.

"Thanks," Jason and I say in unison. We munch on the sugary things as we move about the camp making gestures to comment on good dugout walls and strongly staked tents. Eri eagerly shows us his favorite cooking utensils.

Chuck comes out of the tent with a first aid kit tucked under his arm. "I listened to his chest and heard a gurgling noise in the lower left lung."

Inoki appears with strong, athletic looking Nomo beside him, clinging to his arm. To his team Inoki speaks in Japanese and seems to go on explaining details.

Chuck's blue eyes give off a grim look and tells us, "He's probably telling them about coughed-up blood, headache, and dizziness. Pulmonary edema has set in."

"Can anything be done?" I ask.

"Only one thing," Chuck says.

"Like start back down the mountain?" Jason says.

Inoki nods and switches to English. "Chuck tells us it is the only thing that can save his life."

The Japanese team discusses it in a steady stream of strange words. Nomo says first in Japanese, then in English. "I go." He points down the sloping glacier.

Eri barks back in forceful words. Inoki interprets in English, saying, "Eri, who is Nomo's cousin, will escort him down to our 12,000-foot camp where we have buried supplies."

With a cough, Nomo turns a sad face to the unconquered summit then he ducks into a tent. Eri follows him and glances back at us with tear-filled eyes.

"That should work out well for Nomo," Chuck says. "When he gets lower and breathes more oxygen, his symptoms should begin to fade away."

I look at the uneasy faces of Taiko and Inoki and I ask, "Then you two will stick with it and get all the way up to the summit of Denali?".

"Yes, but we are sorry to lose Nomo. He is our most skilled climber who can get through every tough spot the best way. Nomo teaches us a lot."

Chuck looks up from straightening out his first-aid kit. "At this point the biggest challenges on the route are up ahead."

"In that case, Inoki, you and Taiko should join up with us," Jason says in a way that does not surprise me. To his friends, and in the tradition of his whole family, it is natural that he reaches out a helping hand.

"Good idea," I say and look at Chuck.

He delays, looks thoughtful, then smiles and nods his head.

"Ah, thank you. That will be a great help for us," Inoki says then mumbles off words in Japanese and a big smile fills Taiko's face. He grabs Chuck's gloved hand and pumps it up and down like it is some sort of good luck charm.

Chuck chuckles. "If the weather is good tomorrow, we'll head uphill first thing in the morning."

Taiko joins Jason and me in loud hoots and stomping boots.

"We'll be ready," Inoki says.

With that solution, we bid farewell and hike back to our camp. In less than an hour, we see Eri and Nomo roped together and starting on the downhill route. We talk about weak Nomo who, with Eri's help, will probably sit and scoot down some of the most vertical spots.

The day is spent packing supplies to take and talking about how the summit will be done with two additions to our team. We discuss the pros and cons of taking off in the morning. This camp made us wonder if more rest here will make us strong enough for a heavy one-day push to the summit.

"Since Inoki and Taiko have rested longer at this altitude, they may be more restored and ready than we are," I say.

"Okay, let's see how much energy we all have left after we reach the 17,000 or 18,000 level," Chuck says.

Jason and I are quick to agree.

In the evening, Chuck pulls out the satellite phone and dials his mom in Denver, Colorado. I hear him tell her we are at the spot where horrendous wind made him give up the climb last year. When he hangs up, he hands the phone to Jason.

Jason makes a call to his cousin Frank. When I hear the name Amanda mentioned three times, I glue my ears to his words.

On hang up, I immediately begin taunting him about asking her out. "It's about time you have a date, Jason,"

"Well, how about we double up when you ask Jenny out," he says with a big grin. Then he clobbers my head with a snowball.

I repay with a volley of snowballs to hammer him from head to foot. I don't bother to give him an answer. Dating is tough, and Jenny is way too pretty for me to even speak to her.

"Don't be wimpy, Mitch." I could tell Jason read my thoughts. "If you've got nerve enough to climb this humongous mountain, you can .…."

My snowball hit his cap, leaving his head bare.

I switch to the satellite phone and get through to Ronnie. When I quiz him on what the therapist has him doing, a proud answer comes. "She kept the treadmill off, not moving, and she had me hang on to bars. My leg took some steps, Mitch."

I shower him with praise and start to give him an update on the climb, but I get static feedback followed by a deadline. I chalk it up to the satellite orbiting out of range.

When night comes, so do wicked gusts of wind, but they don't keep me from visualizing awesome Jenny out on the school basketball court. I root for her at the free-throw line, and she gives a shimmering smile that comes right at me. I repeat that dream through the night.

CHAPTER 9

PUSH TO THE SUMMIT

The early morning sky is still half dark when Inoki and Taiko let out whoops as they reach our camp. To keep up with those two early-birds we drag ourselves up, pull on boots, and well-padded parkas. Breakfast is just crackers and energy wheat bars.

Our new Japanese teammates wear yellow backpacks that are as lightweight as the ones we strap on. Eagerness fills their eyes, and our spirits are also high despite the temperature drop to five degrees below zero. In the first light of the clear morning, we rope up together. Chuck takes the lead, Taiko follows, then Jason, Inoki, and I'm last in line.

"Lucky us, we can see the entire range," I holler. "Let's go for it!"

Everyone answers with vigorous shouts.

Our path on crusty snow is a steady uphill slant. Before long, we edge along a snowy granite ridge. There is a steep incline and thin air. That makes us stop to rest after every few steps. It's as if something mysterious is slowing us down. I don't really feel out of breath, just tired. I rest for a minute and feel fine, yet after another few minutes of trudging in such the thin air, I need a break.

Within a couple of hours, we make it to the 17,200-foot altitude and spot an old igloo dug out for a bivouac. We settle down together against snowbanks that shelter us from a strong breeze. We all drink water and dig snacks from our backpacks.

Chuck points toward the route we talked about taking. "That looks like our best route."

Inoki shakes his head and points off to the right. "If we take a straighter line, it will be a shorter and quicker route."

"Yes, but look closely over there," Chuck says. "What do you see?"

"I see a huge column of ice hanging over the trail," I say.

"An avalanche that can come anytime," Chuck says.

"And that could bury us under tons of snow and ice," Jason warns.

With Japanese words to Taiko, Inoki waves his arms like they are caught in an avalanche. With nods they jump to their feet. Inoki grins and says, "Okay, let's go the long way up the mountain."

"This is summit day!" both Jason and I yell as we take off toward the headwall.

The first crevasse we come to has a horrendously wide split. We choose to cross it on a high snow bridge that looks solid. One of us at a time ventures onto it while the rest firmly stake the rope on an anchor. The bridge does not collapse. We get across.

Next, we tackle a long, icy headwall with a slow traverse. After a few steps, we jam in our ice axes and lean on them to rest. We catch our breath and then repeat that routine until we make it to the top of the ridge.

"Right here is Denali Pass at the 18,200-foot level," Chuck announces. He pulls off his backpack and plops down beside a hunk of granite. As each of us catch up to him, we do the same. Rocks help block us from a sweeping wind as we settle in and feast on pieces of dried fish that Taiko passes around.

Taiko takes off his boots and snuggles his cold feet into armpits under Inoki's jacket. No doubt his cold feet lost all feeling. I saw him do some stumbling along the ridge. They talk to each other in unknown words and curiously stare at Jason who gazes up at a dramatic hunk of granite jutting into the blue sky.

"Is that the Archdeacon's Tower that I've read about?" Inoki asks.

"Yes. In the first expedition, Archdeacon Stuck insisted that my great, great uncle Walter Harper be the first man to stand on the summit. That is because the highest mountain looks down upon the land that is an ancient part of our Native life."

"We are in special company." Inoki bows his head in respect then gives the news to Taiko in Japanese. Taiko also bows.

Jason chuckles then hands them some of his favorite pilot bread. Both give the big, white crackers a look of surprise but do not hesitate to bite into them.

Chuck raises a tired voice, "Should we camp right here for a long rest?"

I jump up. "No, let's not stay longer than it takes to snap a few pictures." I yank out my camera and start clicking away.

"Ah, yes. Good to hike on," says Inoki. He helps Taiko get his warmed-up toes back into boots.

"A tough two thousand feet to go, but the weather favors us," Chuck says and struggles to stand up.

As we climb around granite protruding out of snow, I feel a headache coming on. I know it's caused by hard work in extreme high altitude.

In a while we pass by the Archdeacon Tower that tops out at 19,500 feet. I notice Chuck staggers some and he unhooks himself from the rope.

"See the summit. It's under pure blue sky," Jason hollers at him.

Chuck sits down. "My head is hurting so I need a little rest. You go on without me."

We all gather around him and know lack of oxygen in the thin air is playing tricks on his mind and body. Jason says, "I'll take you back down to the camp, Chuck."

"I insist you go on. I'll be okay."

I gasp. "Oh no, Chuck. You're going up to the top with us. It's only 800 feet straight up to the summit."

Jason and I pull him to his feet and strip off his heavy backpack. We hook him back onto the line. Chuck mumbles, "Okay."

All of us decide to lighten up and pile our backpacks on the snow. With my head hurting, too, I'm glad Jason takes the lead.

On the sidewall we need to traverse to the right, a short way from the summit. Together, we take five steps, rest, five more steps, rest, again and again. After every stop, I give a tug on the rope to get Chuck going. He looks dazed by the unfriendly, airless mountain.

When we reach the last one-hundred feet to the summit, we belay each other. One man at a time we make it to the top. First is Jason, our Native Alaskan.

Last is Chuck. Up his last few feet, I pull extra hard on our rope.

"Are we there?" he asks with a puff and pulls off half frost-covered goggles.

"Yes!" We all yell. Surprise fills Chuck's face. He grins and signs of stress wash away.

Right there on Denali Summit we spy the large earth shaped U.S.G.S. marker and put our hands on it before taking snapshots. Standing there, we gaze miles below us at a white-capped world of gigantic mountains. Kahiltna Glacier spreads like a frozen river running fifty miles away.

"We see more than from any seat in an airplane," I say and turn around and around in a circle. "Here we stand right on top of it all!"

All sides of the world roll over thousands of peaks, and valleys stretch to the horizon. Our world gets clicks from cameras and the sound of thankful prayers in two languages.

All I manage to say is, "Thank you, God." I say that over and over.

Inoki raises a glove in a salute and his hoarse voice says, "Here's to Nomo and Eri. We climbed the summit for them too."

I fish out the miniature Alaska flag and stab it into crisp snow. "Here's a hoorah for Ronnie Saunders!"

Jason raises both arms to the sky. "Here's to my Uncle Walter Harper, the first to see the world from the top of Denali!"

Our victory gleams on every face, and we give each other hearty slaps on the back. Yet, we each know that lingering a long time on the summit might invite disaster.

After only a few minutes on top, Jason takes the first downhill step, Taiko nods and follows. Next on the line of rope are Inoki, then Chuck, and I'm last in line.

Exhilaration gives us energy, but so does the downhill motion. To slide takes so much less effort than trudging uphill. Leading us, Jason sets each T-shaped snow anchor that our long rope runs through. Using those and digging our ice axes into the slope keeps us from toppling head over heels off cliffs or sliding into crevasses.

Being last in line, I pull the snow anchors I come to, and Jason waits at the last one until we all meet then takes them to plant on the next steep incline. When we reach the Archdeacon Tower, we stop only long enough to pick up our backpacks.

Minutes later, we make it down to the 18,200 level and I notice the stagger is completely gone from Chuck's legs.

"My head's come back. Not much ache anymore and it's letting me think." Chuck's smile sparkles across whiskers that are white with frost.

"Let's drink to that," I say and hand Chuck a bottle of water. Everyone laughs loudly like that's a funny joke, so I decide I'm not the only one with a light head.

As orange colors from the setting sun shoot through layers of clouds, we spot two climbers passing across the plateau. "Saluto," they call without slowing their stride on the hard, crusty surface.

"Hello," we call and watch what looks like two climbers heading for the summit.

"What country?" Jason asks.

Inoki is quick to say, "Italy, I'm sure. See how they don't rope together."

Chuck wags his head like a disapproving professor. "Rangers say that's not unusual for some European climbers."

"They look tough, but that's still scary," I say and hear Inoki saying a Japanese translation for Taiko.

We descend the wall cautiously using snow anchors to catch any of us who might stumble. In a fairly short time, we reach the long flat across the glacier that leads to our camp. Inoki tells us they will stop by in the morning, and he and Taiko head toward their tent a hundred yards away.

At our camp, Jason and I get our cooker going. With the sun slipping below the horizon, we are more than ready for chow and to sack out in exhaustion. We relish the thought of getting back down to easier breathing at lower altitudes. I hold up crossed fingers for good weather tomorrow to help take us over half the way down off the great mountain.

CHAPTER 10

STRUGGLE TO THE END

A helicopter wakes us up. I crawl out of the tent into sunshine on snow that's too brilliant to see anything. I squint over the ridge and see Inoki and Taiko coming with big packs on their backs. Their heads are tilted up at a helicopter roaring overhead.

"Chuck, Jason, get out here," I shout. "The chopper has a basket hanging from it."

Our tent rocks back and forth as Chuck scrambles to exit. "That has to mean a rescue."

The chopper swoops down the east side of Kahiltna Glacier. "Looks like it is headed right at Windy Corner," Jason says as he steps into sunshine.

"That basket has to be hanging a couple hundred feet below it," Chuck says.

"Hello, hello," is called from both Inoki and Taiko. As they reach us, Taiko hands out strips of smoked fish. It's obvious they are fully packed up and heading down the glacier. Inoki tells us they hope to catch up with Eri and Nomo at their 14,000-foot level base camp. He asks what we might think about the helicopter that we can still hear but no longer see.

"Someone must have taken a terrible tumble," I say.

"No doubt. The hope is to set that suspended basket in a feasible spot where a climber can enter it," Chuck says. He rests a bare hand on Inoki's well padded shoulder. "Now, I hope you will exercise caution, so a rescue won't be needed for your team."

In both languages, our Japanese partners assure Chuck they will. We thank them for giving us a tasty start on breakfast and we shake hands in farewell.

Watching them start down the shimmering glacier, I notice how different it looks this morning. Unlike the wavy sea-of-ice I saw from the summit, at this lower level the glacier looks like ocean breakers filled with pockets big enough to hold freight cars.

"Pilot bread and smoked fish this morning," Jason says.

"Okay," says Chuck. "At our next camp, there's cache we can unbury for a really good lunch."

"Great, let's pack up and start down the mountain." I feel clear-headed and raring to go.

Since the weather is perfect, that's exactly what we do. Wearing so much gear makes the strong sun feels hot, although the temperature is just ten degrees. Our sharp-edged crampons attached to boots dig into the slick, icy surface. That lets us move downhill fast.

Roped together, we again use snow anchors on steep inclines and keep our axes out, ready to stop a slide. Before leaping across crevasses, we take time to cautiously judge the width of the openings.

Like Jason my body seems to be shrinking thin. Constant climbing burns calories off quickly and my appetite had faded in the highest altitudes, but as we descend, I start feeling hungry again. When we stop for snacks, my stomach grumbles for food. All three of us dig in for lunch.

By late afternoon, we come face to face with the Fat Dog sculpture I had chiseled out of ice to mark our cache at 14,200 feet. The plateau holds several group camps, including our four Japanese friends. We greet them, then we meet two women climbers from Washington, three men from Germany, and a group of five from

Ireland. All of them plan to head up toward the summit of the big mountain.

As soon as we are set up for the night, Chuck gets a call in to Radio Sally. Very little of what I hear him say has anything to do with us standing on Denali summit. Noticeable excitement in his voice seems to center on her promise to meet our train. When he sees me staring at him with open ears, his swishing hand shoos me away.

After Jason puts in a call to his family with news of our victory, I call my folks. I put off calling Ronnie. I want to wait until we fly to Talkeetna in just a couple more days. I guess that's because I want to let him know when all our danger is conquered.

As we greeted other climbers their comments focused on the rescue helicopter. To our horror, we learn of a fatal fall off Denali Pass by a climber from Italy. He had stumbled on the icy ridge and fell over 1,000 feet. His partner was able to climb down to him, and he stayed with him through a cold night without a tent until a helicopter could respond. Chuck, Jason, and I are certain they are the two Italian men who passed by us yesterday.

With all campers, conversations on that subject linger into the night. Chuck gives advice about using ropes and snow anchors especially when inclines steep with 45 to 50 degrees. He warns against cold temperatures, high winds, extreme altitude headaches and fatigue. While Chuck gets deep into giving tips and answers questions about how we use T-shaped aluminum snow anchors, Jason and I retreat toward our tent.

Under a full moon and a star studded black sky, our thoughts are on the tragic loss of the climber. We pause for a silent prayer. In a somber mood, we collapse into our sleeping bags.

Above a whistling wind, Jason asks, "What's going to be your next challenge, Mitch?"

A powerful urge to be completely honest struck me. "I'm going to ask Jenny out."

"Brave move! Let's make it a double date. You and Jenny see a movie with me and Amanda."

We both start laughing. The laugh goes on and on. I try to smother mine with the sleeping bag over my head, but gagging laughs keep coming and linger until every ounce of energy melts me. Tears of relief spill. I attribute that to conquering the summit and hearing the sad fate of a climber. Also, I wonder if such a smart girl as Jenny would let me touch her glossy hair that hangs all the way down to her hips. Finally, howling gusts of wind that flap against the tent drown out my thoughts. I fall asleep.

****

In the morning, a big bowl of hot oatmeal tastes good. Without any delay, we rig up and set out for the cache where the sleds are stored. We put on wool face masks as a stinging wind hits us head on, but the hike down to the 12,900 level moves along smoothly. Luckily, we find our old campsite still had a good barrier for shelter from the wind. In our stashed supplies I find a can of mixed nuts. All three of us munch on nuts like they are pure luxury.

We hustle to get the sleds packed up with loads strapped on tightly and clip them on the rope. Then the old battle begins. Like dogs anxious to run downhill, the sleds sometimes shoot past us or give us a yank. A sled slips around Jason's legs. He trips and falls with a splat face down. I whip out my camera for quick shots that guarantee I can show for a laugh at a party.

The Ozone sculpture we had done for our 11,000-foot bivouac is loaded with new snow. Jason and I cannot resist knocking the big Ozone over before we continue downhill. Soft snow requires snowshoes, but we keep up a good pace most of the afternoon. The sleds become easier to control on a more gradual slope.

It is a happy sight when we reach our first campsite at the 7,900-foot level. Now we're only a few hundred yards from the landing field. Chuck gets on the phone to K2 Flight Service, and we learn we'll be the first team aboard in the morning.

All evening we mix with other climbers camped there. Details about the miraculous helicopter pilot managing the rescue are discussed, and, again, eager ears listen to Chuck's detailed safety advice.

When we settle into our tent, Chuck asks, "Jason, how did you feel about following in your great, grand uncle's path to conquer North America's highest summit?"

"Back in those days, Walter Harper had a lot harder climb to become the first man, a Native, to stand on top of Denali Mountain. I'm even more proud of him than I ever was." Jason's eyes widen with pride.

Chuck pounds him on his back, and I give him a high five.

"This year our team reached the top of the summit. But Jason, you were first climber, our summit leader," I say.

"Back in 1913 dogsleds were the only way for the Archdeacon party to get to the foot of the mountain and home again." Jason goes on telling how someone his age, a native boy, was camped with the dogs at about a 3,000-foot level. He had waited there alone for many weeks believing the expedition would someday return. When they finally did, the young boy provided them with food, tents, and dog sleds for the long drive home to the city of Fairbanks.

We listen to his story while we eat lots of fresh popped popcorn. Then we play a few hands of cards until light goes out of the sky.

****

In a clear and breezy morning, we tromp fully loaded with our gear to the airstrip. Our wait is short before the bright red plane appears. The pilot is the same. Duke gives us a wave as the airplane's skies touch snow, and taxis to a stop on the wind-swept glacier.

"Make it to the top?" Pilot Duke calls out as two passengers disembark.

Questions pour from them as they grab their climbing gear. Their congratulations and praise are real music to us. Chuck stays quiet while Jason and I brag about being conquerors of the big mountain. Our chests puff up and stick out.

"Put your bags on board the plane," Duke yells.

As we lift our gear up, we bid our audience a good and safe climb. We follow Chuck, carrying gear, and hustle into the plane. Duke revs the engine and heads the nose of the plane into the wind. On a bumpy run we have a good take off.

Soaring above Kahiltna Glacier we get a view of grand whiteness sprinkled with bright colored tents set up by climbers. The summit on

Denali cannot be seen behind thick clouds. A grey mist also envelops Mt. Foraker. Snow drifts in mighty winds off Mt. Huntington. All this shows climbers will face weather that promises to change again and again.

Before long we see color green below us sweeping over trees and the valley floor. Duke brings us down for a smooth landing in Talkeetna.

When Duke gets us unloaded at the airfield, a half-dozen eager climbers shower us with questions. I leave Chuck and Jason with them.

Alone, I sit atop my backpack in a sunny spot. Digging deep into a bag I pull out my cell phone, dial and count the rings until Ronnie answers.

'That you, Mitch?"

"We're here, down in the town of Talkeetna."

"What happened?"

"A lot happened, but we made to the summit of Mount Denali." I soak up his shouts of joy. When I promise lots of pictures, his squealing simmers down. I ask, "How is it you're doing?"

"Mitch, guess what." He doesn't wait for my guess. "Johnnie got me a leg made of metal and plastic. She strapped it on me, and I stood right up. She said one of these days I won't have to hang on to anything, and I can learn to run. How's that?"

I choke up and can't speak.

"Mitch, did you hear me?"

I clear my throat and manage to say, "You are the big winner, Ronnie!"

END

ABOUT THE AUTHOR

Marie Osburn Reid has enjoyed watching changes take place in Alaska since it became a state in 1959. After a college degree at Chico State University, she moved from Truckee, California to the Land-of-the-Midnight Sun in 1958. In Fairbanks, Alaska she and her first husband, Austin G. Ward, raised three children, Marci, Mitchell, and Merrick. Her first publications were two stories in *Highlights for Children* magazine under her former name Marie Delilah Ward.

After retiring from employment at the University of Alaska Museum of the North in 2005, she married her long-ago, high school boyfriend, Reford (Jeep) Reid. They continue to enjoy winter and summer activities in Alaska, and she has taken up novel writing.

The cover picture on "Climbing the Great Denali" was one taken of her son Mitchell Ward on his mountain climb. He is an expert mountaineer and gave his mother great help in contributing true facts for this story.

Each of the following books are perfect for readers of about 6th grade and up.

YOUNG ADULT NOVELS
by
MARIE OSBURN REID

THE SPIRIT BASKET portrays historical events experienced by an Alaska Native family over 270 years. In various locations in Alaska, generations of teenagers adjust from subsistence living to invading fur trappers, the purchase of Alaska from Russia, gold-rush fever, WWII detention, huge earthquake, disastrous oil spill and much more. Beginning in 1745, each chapter tells an adventure by a new generation of the same family. The story ends in the year 2015.

OVER RAINBOWS is a mystery in early Alaska! An orphaned young girl tells of sailing to Alaska in 1925 to fulfill their father's dying wish. Her sister is promised to be the bride of a wealthy gold miner. An evil force follows them on sea, land, and in the air as they work to solve a murder. Their lives revolve around a bush pilot, pioneer, mystic, gambler, and friends. Inspired by the thrill of aviation, their adventure brings life-threatening danger and sparks of love. This is an exciting novel for anyone who enjoys a fast-moving mystery.

WHISPERS TO A DEAF DOG A bear attacks, ice on the Yukon River breaks open, a mother moose charges, races begin for energetic sled dogs. A very special dog leads the way and saves lives. Experiences are either told by James or by Brooke Anne. Their adventures as teenagers bring danger, outstanding dogs, tests of culture, and a glimpse of lives evolving. This novel is exciting for anyone who loves a dog and wants to know about racing sled dogs.

CLIMBING THE GREAT DENALI is fiction based greatly on a journal kept by the author's son, Mitchell Austin Ward, the second time he climbed Denali (Mt. McKinley).

All books appeal most to sixth graders and up. Each is available online from Amazon or Barnes & Noble. Each book is in paperback or Kindle e-books.

Book reprint, edited by author in 2023

Made in the USA
Middletown, DE
05 March 2023

26168115R10080